W9-CER-451

How Things Are Made

Milk to Ice Cream

By Inez Snyder

Welcome Books™

SCHOLASTIC INC.

New York Toronto London Auckland Sydney
Mexico City New Delhi Hong Kong Buenos Aires

Photo Credits: Cover and all photos by Maura B. McConnell
Contributing Editor: Jennifer Silate
Book Design: Mindy Liu

No part of this publication may be reproduced in whole or in part,
or stored in a retrieval system, or transmitted in any form or by any means,
electronic, mechanical, photocopying, recording, or otherwise,
without written permission of the publisher. For information regarding permission,
write to Scholastic Inc., Attention: Permissions Department,
557 Broadway, New York, NY 10012.

ISBN 0-516-24451-5

Copyright © 2003 by Rosen Book Works, Inc. All rights reserved.
Published by Scholastic Inc. SCHOLASTIC and associated logos are
trademarks and/or registered trademarks of Scholastic Inc.

12 11 10 9 8 7 6 5 4 3   4 5 6 7 8 /0

Printed in the U.S.A.   61

First Scholastic paperback printing, October 2003

Contents

Hi, my name is Mark.

My dad and I are going
to make **ice cream**.

We use milk to make
ice cream.

I mix the milk and some
eggs together in a bowl.

Then, I mix sugar, flour, and salt in another bowl.

Now, Dad and I mix everything together.

Next, Dad cooks
the **mixture**.

He **stirs** the mixture
while it cooks.

The mixture is finished cooking.

Dad puts in some **cream**.

I add **vanilla** to the mixture.

Vanilla will make the
ice cream taste good.

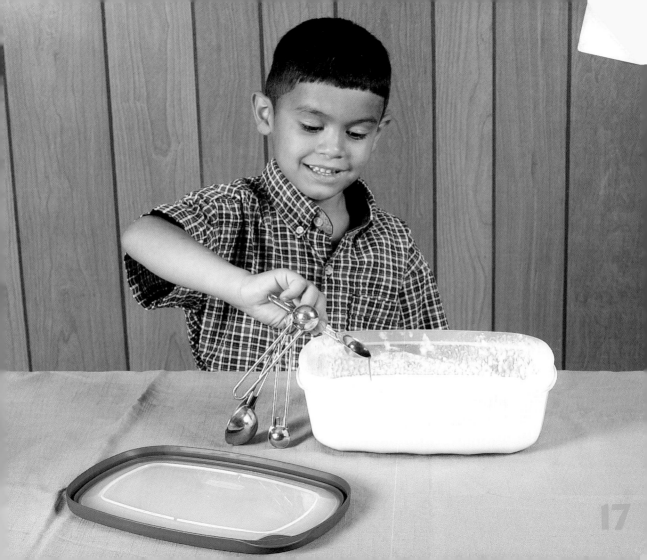

Now, Dad puts the mixture in the **freezer**.

Soon, it will be ice cream.

The ice cream is finished.

It tastes great!

New Words

cream (**kreem**) a thick, fatty liquid found in whole milk

freezer (**free**-zur) the part of a refrigerator that makes food icy or solid

ice cream (**ise kreem**) a frozen food made from milk or cream, sugar or honey, and sometimes eggs

mixture (**miks**-chur) something made from different things mixed together

stirs (**stuhrz**) when someone mixes something by moving it around in a container with a spoon or a stick

vanilla (vuh-**nil**-uh) a flavor that comes from the seed of a plant, and is used in ice cream, cakes, and other foods

To Find Out More

Books
From Cow to Ice Cream
by Bertram T. Knight
Children's Press

Ice Cream
by Jules Older
Charlesbridge Publishing

Web Site
Ice Cream: an Education
http://www.ice-cream.org/school/index.htm
Learn about the history of ice cream and play games on this Web site.

Index

About the Author
Inez Snyder writes and edits children's books. She also enjoys painting and cooking for her family.

Reading Consultants
Kris Flynn, Coordinator, Small School District Literacy, The San Diego County Office of Education

Shelly Forys, Certified Reading Recovery Specialist, W.J. Zahnow Elementary School, Waterloo, IL

Sue McAdams, Former President of the North Texas Reading Council of the IRA, and Early Literacy Consultant, Dallas, TX